Songs of
Seasoned Women

Edited by
Patti Tana

Quadrasoul, Inc.
Long Island City, NY

Quadrasoul, Inc.
4720 Center Blvd., Suite 516
Long Island City, NY 11109
(646) 429-0859

ISBN: 978-0-9787298-3-7 Softcover
ISBN: 978-0-9787298-4-4 Hardcover

Cover art: "Alley Pond," collage, copyright 2000 by Sharon Bourke,
        reprinted with permission of the artist.

Acknowledgments appear in the *About the Poets* & *Acknowledgments*
beginning on page 165 and constitute an extension of this copyright page.

May *Songs of Seasoned Women*
inspire you to sing

Table of Contents

Sacred Space

Grandmother's Veins

I Ate My Mother's Hair

A Small Voice

Philosophy, Romance of the Aged

The Garden

Coda: Seasoned

Eve's Song

Eve's Song

I eat apples.
Honey apples
round as breasts
red as robins,
setting suns:
a serpent didn't tell me
I found them for myself.

And I eat apples
still inside the tree.
My knowledge comes
in wine red spurts
of running sap:
feet sucking earth
limbs branching out
fingers flowering.

I eat apples.
I don't care if I'm thrown out:
they never named
the things I knew,
it never was
my garden.

Sally Ann Drucker

Swallower of Sins

Give me your sweet sins,
give me your round and glorious sins,
your sharp and pointy transgressions,
your broadsword-sized lies,
your loved ones' needs unmet,
the hungry mouths of their demands
pursuing you in your dreams.

Give me your truckload of reasons unvoiced,
your harvest of excuses baled and
scattered across your landscape.
You don't need them.
Give me your swollen and bulbous worries. ·
Give up your knotty-muscled sins,
twisting sour in your belly, their
hot vomitus creeping into your throat
day and night.

Pull those braided, hempen ropes of guilt
right out of your mouth. Open wide.
Their strands scratch past your teeth,
your lips. Let go of them. Do it now.
And I will lay them out, your misshapen bundles
arrayed on the grass. Then,
I will give you a broad grin, a wink,
tilt back my head, spreading my lips wide
and lower your swords of torment one by one into my
commodious throat. One, two, twenty-two,
there — you see? All gone, vanished, devoured.
For I am the swallower of sins.

Barbara Barnard

Riding Past the Museum of Natural History & Seeing the Steps

the steps I first took
toward infidelity — how
far I descended. My lover

is history — has been
for some thirty-odd years.
Still, I remember

the nervous excitement
at first blush. How beautiful
I was, how attentive my soon-

to-be lover. How unashamed
& unnaturally good I felt.
I see the steps past my reflection

in the car window. How beyond
stupid I'd been, thinking I'd scale them
unscathed — so sure I was just

stepping into my husband's footprints — the deepest impressions set
years before I ever thought

I'd venture to make hurt go
away by going the ways
of wayward flesh — before I knew

what I know now: crawl space
one could reach by whittling a niche
in a marriage preserved for the children's sake.

Ruth Sabath Rosenthal

Williamsburg Poem

shaking like the El beneath the Williamsburg train
I wait for him to come
bridge and tunnel meeting like the girders of the El
his hard arms open my thighs

in the hood they have names for him
the girls say his names:
they call him *dos cafes con leche*
they say *ruega para nosotros*
they say he's yucca, white and shining
like the crucifix on your breast
they say he's lucky like a spider
they say he's yucca, white and hard

they watch him
run like a wolf on the rooftops
run like a wolf on the rooftops
every night

rumbling
like the train beneath the sidewalk
and the El above my head
encircled by
these girders and his arms he
whispers spray paint and graffiti
pulls me down into the subway
pulls me down and up again
lifts me to the bridge the girders tattooed light the open El

his mouth burns the asphalt
graffiti burns my thighs
and I run through the clothes lines that flap on the roofs
I run through the night after him

the girls give me garlic
the girls all pray for me
and I pray with the words from the spray-painted walls
and the girders that shake on the El and I pray:
he is my catholic *con leche*
he is my old native religion
I pray: *ruega para nosotros*
I pray: *ruega para mi*

he is my *brujo lobo blanco*
he is my *lobo y arana*
and my prayers are as dark and as deep as your night
as the hole he will fill with his eyes
here in me

laughing
he opens
my Williamsburg thighs

Larissa Shmailo

Wolf Season

I smelled your wolf scent on the wind
and knew your wheels had touched ground.

Brother wolf, so many seasons absent,
come walk with me. The woods beckon
just ahead. I trot, behind you at first.
Then we are side by side on the narrow path,
our flanks touching. I nudge my muzzle into
the thick fur between your shoulder blades as
we make our way down the path. There is
more gray in your pelt now than the last time.
It becomes you. Now we are running and you
ease out ahead of me on the path; trees guide
up on either side. We stretch our legs and glide
easily over a fallen log, its bark laced with
green lichen.

We burst suddenly out of trees, into a sun drenched
clearing, our tails wagging. We play tag
a while in the meadow, tossing a stick, chewing
fallen tree branches. Then we stop, panting, to
rest. We lie down in a scattering of wildflowers —
purple, yellow, brightest blue. Our muzzles touch
and we remember other seasons. You doze briefly,
your paws twitching with the dream of the hunt.
Your breath comes fast as storms when you bring down
your prey. Bees make a warm buzz visiting the flowers.
The sun drops lower in the sky, over the treetops;
suddenly, the hum of a cicada becomes
the roar of a jet, lofting above our forest.
My heart contracts.

Barbara Barnard

Small Galaxy

We worked long and hard,
the world and I, for this place —
cool and warm in shifts
just reward after thunder.

The sky too clear to trust
I placed my stars
in my own galaxy.

They ran through my hair at night
dripping dew on my breast
salve for what might have been.

Now I must come down
taking the stars along
on a midnight ride to hell.

E. Willa Haas

Tell Me the Truth

Will you walk away from
your fascination with danger?
His blue eyes riveting your body
to the edge of a summer sky,
imploring you to leave everything behind.
The habit of him a hurricane
beating your heart into submission.
His laughter a carnival of joyful madness.

Tell me the truth.
Will you gallop over the fences of logic
just to taste the bittersweet
dripping from his lips?
Will you dive into reefs of confusion,
the rush of his arms
waiting to ingest your desire?

The truth.
Will you spin with him
in the curve of Saturn's ring?
Fly with him
in the yawn of canyon rocks?
Sleep with him
in the blanket of Sahara's dunes?
Will the persuasion of his blue eyes wane
like the chill of a bone white moon?

Sasha Ettinger

Serving Notice

Know that there is one
Old Lady left on earth
Who has been close enough to death
To taste the hotness of his breath

Know that the old Lady
Dreams of dancing with the devil
When she dies

Know you that the devil
Is that handsome one
That one who she once so loved
The devil with his tight blue jeans still on

No delicate two-step
They waltzed to the boogie beat
Oh how they strutted and they strolled
Dirty dancing all the way
To the grand march at the last spring ball
The one where they horrified all
The chaperones
Got themselves warned then
Got themselves banned from the DAR hall

Oh yes know that the devil can
Be prince charming
Boyishly disarming
Steal your heart
Take it with him
Even when he dies

Beverly E. Kotch

The Wife of God II

One night when He is late (again)
and she has too much time to spend
lighting meteors, mending
black holes in the universe,
she looks out at the vast array
of planets and of atoms and says
Hey! I am creative too.
Ex nihilo, out of the blue She
never knew belonged to Her,
She spins a sky so high and wide
the angels have to look up to admire.
And under it She rolls a globe
of steamy seas and fragrant stone
and clouds of fire.
And though She knows He'll be chagrined,
that She will have to face His wrath,
then (God forbid!) His impotence,
out of thin air She pulls
the first fine strands of life:
its single cells have wings.
It is no sin to be original, She says,
and as She makes it all begin
for the first time in eternity
She sings.

Susan Astor

Skin Knows Skin

Skin Knows Skin

The way the water spreads beneath the wind
　　across the pond in widening waves
　　　　of sparkling light —
the way a sleek, elegant animal arches
　　into the palm of a familiar
　　　　beloved hand —
I tremble beneath your touch.

How can the body respond
　　year after year
　　　　to the same urges and delights?
Skin knows skin
　　I say when you press into my body
　　　　soft flesh and hard bones.
Skin loves skin
　　your body replies
　　　　stretched head to toe beside.

Patti Tana

I Love You Again for the First Time

When at last we're in the same city
Then in the same building
Finally in the same room
After twenty-five years
You stride to me without hesitation.
I stretch for your cool neck,
Stand taller to find the spot
Behind the ear and we're back
At the dance.

The gym floor feels hot
From your game.
The heat rises through my socks
Up my legs and into the muscles of my back
Where your hands are spread.
They're called good hands
Athletic and smart.

You do not bend for me; I lift to you.
Our hips hold fast so I can lead you;
I'm your first.
I coax you to be slow and real, to relax
So your hand will fall to the small of my back
Where it presses. . .

We sway and sway
Long after the music has stopped.

Susan Melchior

Hands Rough as Bark

Gleaming mahogany slips
Falls to the floor with a hollow thud,
Leaving splinters in its wake.

But a carpenter knows
How to create beauty
Out of unvarnished wood.

He can snap a level line
When the floor dips away
Into the darkest corners of nothingness.

He can hold a tiny fragment of a table leg
In hands rough as bark
With exquisite grace.

The orphan piece
Torn so rudely from its brethren
Lies almost motionless in his gentle fingers.

Like some wild, wounded creature,
It knows instinctively
To trust such tender ministrations.

A bit of glue applied with deftness
Perfects the union and balances the whole
So it can bear the weight.

Beverly Weisman

If I Were to Come Across You on a Rainy Night

If I were to come across you
on a rainy night
spouting poetry under a damp umbrella
or splashing through a river of syllables
I would stop
and place my ear to your lips
absorb the ripple of your voice
and the soft pitty pat of phrases
dancing off the roof

If I were to come across you on a rainy night
drizzling letters on my glass pane
in a dark or lyrical rhythm
I would throw open the window
and drink in the vapor

but I am dry at home
sniffing at the moist night air
like one of my dogs
and dreaming of being a landscape
bathed in a sea of mist
or a mountain under your cloud
waiting for a shower
of words

Jennifer Rosoff

Then Again

Yesterday I was the rain on the roof
when all the doors were locked
and no one was home to let me in.

The wind was cold. I heard an owl.

I remembered the time you rose,
opened the window where I waited,
repeating myself till dawn.

But that was another yesterday.
A warm night when I was falling
and you were catching me.

Linda Opyr

I See Your Face

when your face
is not before me.
It slips behind
my eyes and
travels my body
in paths felt,
not seen.

When I bring
the lilac
to my lips,
it is there.
And spring
is a kiss
more breath
than touch.

When I press
my palms
to the sand,
it is there.
And night
is a whisper
more skin
than sound.

I feel your face
when your face
is not before me.
It slips around
my shoulders and
closes my eyes
with hands seen,
not felt.
And my body
is liquid.
And my eyes,
hands.

And touch,
the glimpse
of your face
before me.

Linda Opyr

Ground Fires at Cedar Point

On the road to Cedar Point
we sat beneath the shadow
of Saint Anne's cross
eating shrimp and bread.

Later we drifted the tidal
flow at Cedar Point,
amazed the water was still clear.

All around us, sand dunes
ripe with honeysuckle,
blossoms yellow as Irish butter,
white as winter moon.

We hid ourselves behind
the flowered vines, dried
our bodies, smoothed the towel
across our necks and thighs,
the place where lovers kiss

in perfect stillness —
the sound of cloth on anointed skin.

Gladys Henderson

Washday

everyone used to hang laundry
to dry in the fresh air
great looping clotheslines
held sheets full and fat
as Spanish galleons

each line told its tale
of diapers, dungarees
and lingerie hung
for the sun to sanitize

I hung my panties in the sun
neatly
by the waistband,
not like my hot-blooded neighbor
who smiled the crotch to catch
the brightest rays

inviting ultra violet
to disinfect the cloth
that touched the places
the nuns would never name.

Barbara Reiher-Meyers

Women in Love

Hip to hip
they whisper in the kitchen
while in the den
the men talk shop.

Arm in arm
they linger in the garden
until their shadows
round out into one.

They do not have to learn
each other's curves;
they know.

Later, they will intertwine
for hours on the phone
as the wash goes through its cycles
as the children have their baths.
So simple, it is almost laughable
this bliss of being more than sisters.
How could anyone object?

Susan Astor

Let's Stay

Let's stay as we are, my Love
Our own god in plastic skin
Settled into fancy paradoxes
We believe to be just.

Do not alter my imbalances
Clothed in dreams
Of perfect tomorrows.
Uncertainty must remain.

Just please stay
Warm in your nearness
Solid in concern
Accepting my differences

As beauty
Maybe mystery.

E. Willa Haas

Black Beauty

Black beauty so undefined and misunderstood
Associated with the unknown lost culture of African tales
Depicted as crack heads and whores.
Who knows what black beauty truly is? What makes me?
Stereotyped to have a big butt, ebony skin, and bad weave
But I will tell you what makes me a true beauty.
I could care less what the fool next to you said
I will tell what black beauty is...
It is the stride of a tall chocolate woman,
Light or dark
It is the smile of a small child with dark shiny black hair
And a bright smile that could make you begin to tear.
I will tell you black beauty is no thing of the past.
It is alive and grows within the souls of all
Not meant to be mocked
Dare not mistake it, or disrespect it.
Founded in the beat of the African plains
Innate in the stature of Egyptian Kings and Queens
It comprises the beautiful and diverse race I come from.
I will tell you what makes me!
It is the words of poetry and truth I speak
It is the innocence and loudness that fill my laughter
It is the brown chocolate eyes that I see the world through
It is the caramel brown soft skin that my body is covered in
It is the small hands and ears I have and giggle about
And my black woman shape
You shouldn't assume but appreciate
It is my feet that take me far into this rough world
For I will tell you what makes me...
It is everything you don't have and hate me for
For there is only one me.
Black beauty is all around. Just look and you will see
That's what makes me.

Natasha M. Ewart

Bending to Her Bath

she thinks of him
how she will fill him with herself,
how he will rise to take her in.

Slowly, she extends a foot into the tub;
she does not want the pleasure all at once.

The warm is strong;
it rolls along the low slope of her calf.

And now she half-submits.
She sits and lets the water find its way.

She stays and stays,
then bows to lean her breasts
against the clear seam of the surface:
she dreams it is his mouth.

Gently she slides back
to rest her head against the porcelain.
She feels the wet touch on her neck,
the water lick her lip.

How patient she is now,
how well-prepared.
Her body is a prayer she knows he'll answer.

Susan Astor

What She Knows

A man has planted something
far inside me, an image or a form,
brown seed, word, deed — all things
become the same in this chamber —
and since the time he planted it
a dreamy rush of pleasure

has taken hold. First of my heart,
pumping all the while my own
blood, pumping through my veins
into my brain into the textured
lining of my lungs where
song is born,

pressing through my breasts,
rounded nipples, flowing hips, desire
in my belly running idly down my thighs.
I part my legs and touch myself:
is this the magic of translation
or his hand?

A searing rod or root keeps re-entering
my flesh *my language is my body I am
very much alive.*

Pat Falk

A Clean Wound

A Clean Wound

My words are dog eared
from indifferent thumbings,
shopworn from being too long
in the bargain basement.

I filter love through a screen
of sorry wisdom, mangled,
passed through a mind armed
with barricades, suspicions.

Still I believe love a clean wound,
a constant letting of the soul,
free blowing ribbon of satin,
blood soaked, proud.

There, a fire tries to burn
without smudge of shame.
Can I be born anew,
emerge pure and gleaming,
lovable as a child is lovable?

Then.

Evelyn Kandel

The Compact

He brought it home from Japan, from the airport
at Narita, a last minute gift. I understand that,
the last minute shift in consciousness, when you begin
to think of where you are going, that nether space
before departure, where fluorescent lights insist
you remember what is forgotten. At Narita,
on the outskirts of Tokyo, there exists
time and obligation and you.

He bought the baby a dog that barked and wagged its tail
when he'd clap his powerful hands, until time would
stop its batteries and the sound of those hands. For me,
a compact with delicate inlaid gold leaves and stems,
white flowers blooming against the profoundness
of black, its latch rimmed in silver with an infinity
of etched diamond shapes spiraling on the back
where it fits in the palm of the hand.

It held no powder. I loved this compact,
more beautiful than I could bear. At one time I filled it.
Now residues cover the mirrored insides, I see myself
through its soft haze. We have both rusted. Here
age has crept about, pitting and pocking roundness.
Yet, I cannot discard this gift, as I have the giver.
I no longer see the depth in his chiseled brow,
overgrown with frown. Perhaps my eyes fail me.

I remember so little of us. Fragments mostly —
more rote, the way I remember *Columbus*
sailed the ocean blue in 1492. But not love,
not passion, afterimages telescoped, tiny and distant.
How can such intensity be but a shadow,
a boat on the ocean ringed and reduced by the horizon?
Time compresses everything. As you get closer to death
this moment recedes. In its stead, the past emerges.

Will I call you husband again?
Who might I call to in the darkness of night,
the past or the present? Within the compact's
dusty mirror, time stretches untelling.
When the moment arrives, I will have long buried
the questions and perhaps the compact with its inlay of gold,
delicate white flowers, and the infinite spiraling of diamonds,
more beautiful than I can bear.

Mallic E. Boman

The Waiting Room

Someone from London looks up from his laptop.
Someone from New York looks up from her book.
There is recognition, something familiar, yet uncertain.
One never knows if the familiarity is a reminder,
someone else, a prior life of sorts.
He wears a wedding band. She wears a wedding band.
They sit waiting to embark on a journey.
He is starting out.
She is catching the connecting flight.
He thinks, perhaps they will be seated next
to each other, or adjacent in some way.
She thinks, there is no chance they can be
seated next to each other, he must be
first-class, she is economy cabin.
Nothing will happen. Everything can happen.
She wonders if there's time to brush her teeth again
against the acrid taste of flying all night.
A delay announcement blares
from the tiled ceiling. He gets a call
just as he contemplates a cup of coffee.
She closes her book, heads for a cappuccino.
There are glances. She returns. And it is over.
Seating rows 22 through 34.
Leaving one airless place for another,
she rises and boards. They will not meet again.
Nothing has happened. Too much has happened.

Mallie E. Boman

Thin Silk Dress

Gradually, the day wears on
　　to the place it might have been.

Or, would it then have turned just so
　　I have no certain way to know.

Rutty road in either case
　　no daisy path for me.

Winter stock in thin silk dress
　　surprised at what might be.

E. Willa Haas

For Want of Red

"I want a red dress.
I want it flimsy and cheap
I want it too tight, I want...."
Kim Addonizio, *"What Do Women Want?"*

I see men wanting a red-clad woman:
see-through-cheap red — backless
& sleeveless, breast-tight, cheek-taut.

Behind their ogling, no thoughts barred;
what ecstasy, peeling her ruby-ripe layers,
her glistening core color revealed. O!

to see the body in red slink past
"All You Can Eat" to "The Pink Pussy"
down the street; to nosedive into hard-

core fantasy, rock & roll in it. Hey,
in the thick of it all, they appear master-
fully cool — cucumbers that'll escape

getting caught red-handed eyeballing
the eye-catcher. In the dogged pursuit
of red, each voyeur cocksure of coming

home fulfilled, no shred of red
showing — my old man, a looker
from way back, home to me, his post-

menopausal wife, whose red faded
dress grows threadbare, wizened eyes
chronically bloodshot bawling over this

most wearing state of affairs. I look
to my husband to redress despair,
hold me, at the very least, notice me.

He looks my way — turns away.

Ruth Sabath Rosenthal

Thaw

The glacier recedes,
leaving tides high
and dangerous
and striations on the land,
tracking.

We have not spoken to each other
these many weeks,
occupying accompanying space,
repelling like the same-charged polarity
we were.
Sparks no long flew.
It was the cold time,
winter of the soul,
all soft sentiment turned hard
and breakable,
easy to shatter.
And we stood in that thin sheet of slippery surface,
each convinced of walking-on-water rectitude
while our weight fissured the glaze.
We stood our sinking ground
resolutely.

I do not know what changed our minds.
Perhaps it was not quite being able to remember
what started it
this time.
Perhaps it was just becoming too easy
to slither past the other.
Perhaps it was the mirrors
we'd turned to the wall.

This morning I made your coffee
and buttered your toast.
This morning your shower towel
wasn't on the bathroom floor.
This morning we saw our reflection
in each other.

Perhaps it was the fear
of what we were sliding into
that pulled us back.

And the glacier recedes,
leaving tides high
and dangerous
and striations on the land,
tracking.

Barbara Novack

Bathysphere

Today I'm remembering the story you told me
about the crying divers — strong men, highly
trained in the skills of deep sea diving,
fit and ready as Navy Seals. But who can
fathom the mysteries of the deep? You'd
seen them, more than once, emerge from a
long dive beneath earth's fragile, watery
sheath. You'd seen them remove their tanks,
their masks, the red diver-down flag
lowered. The divers would sit at rest, in their
wet suits, arms slack, heads bowed.

They've had no problems with breathing
tanks, masks or hostile marine animals
on this dive. All the same, they hang their
heads, catching their breath. One man sobs.
Another's eyes well with tears. Soon they are
all heaving with some waterborne sorrow or
knowledge, some fear or longing unfathomable.
They weep, not ashamed — a shared cleansing.
Later they will drink cups of coffee and
laugh together, a return to air and light
from the stillness of the deep.

But our own descent was not in wet suits with
separate tanks. We were sealed in the bathysphere,
breathing the same air, the same dreams, for a span.
We gave ourselves time to come up, avoiding the bends.
Reemerging, drinking in once again the ordinary air
of life on the surface, we look back once or twice
at the steel ball in which we made our journey. We
kiss, smiling, and begin to swim, our strokes taking
us in different directions once again. Behind my
smile, something catches in my throat and I know
that one thing the divers felt was loss. Like me,
they couldn't put a name to what they'd lost
as they drifted cautiously, almost
reluctantly, back to the surface.

Barbara Barnard

Smokescreen

I forget what you said, I didn't really hear it.
I remember the smoke rising
from the wood chips, it swathed you,
made you resemble a dream, undefined
yet large as life.
Your hands open on the stone,
I remember them, white against the gray.

You were so intent,
I wish I knew what you were telling.
I kept looking,
heard the sound of your voice,
the low baritone of your laughter.
I only understood
the trees, the breeze that ruffled your hair.

Perhaps you will write down all you were saying,
words I could see, savor their shapes.
All went so soon — a flight of birds overhead
before I could identify them.
Birds do not matter, but words are
where you live.
I often lose you there.

Let us start again,
it will be different, I will watch your lips,
move closer to you
on the other side of the smoke
that clouds your words.

Diana Festa

When Was I This Alone with Anyone

The burden of your presence
    in your well cut jacket
    that just had to be hung just so,
    followed by absence of conversation
    because you had to unwind,
    stifling the atmosphere with your demand
    that we tiptoe around you.

When you finally deigned to join us,
    you darkened the light
    with prophecy of our doom.

Mary Himmelweit

Poem for Lady Day

Billy, I write this poem
to tell you
when my man left me
after he broke
my pretty white nose
how I lay
under that blood stained sheet
weeping, weeping
while you, skinny arms
trembling in elbow length gloves
a velvety gardenia
spreading its white palm
in the licorice black of your hair
opened your plum mouth
swallowing me, swallowing me
down, down
into the belly of your blues

Gloria g. Murray

Parting Gifts

Tokens of our erstwhile love
gather dust too quickly,
take up precious room.

I'm sending back the book
of tedious verse pressed
around wilted wildflowers,
the mirror of your self-image
its silver dulled, a pink-lipped
seashell on the mantle
that resonates with your voice,
robs me of my solitude.

I'll just throw out the champagne
bottles of your promises —
some empty, some gone flat —
they're all broken anyway.

What I will keep are the few
crystal moments. They take
up little space, catch light,
toss rainbows against the wall.

What I cannot return
is your letter saying how
concerned you are — as a friend.
When I tore it up, the pieces
just blew away.

Katherine A. Hogan

Too Long Gone

Perhaps you have been gone too long.
The earth that once bore your footprints
Has worn smooth and wouldn't recognize
Your once familiar step.
You, the one who told me how you hated change
Have made the world change on the path behind you,
Have turned the once beloved word "home"
Into "forgotten."
What great adventure have you found out there
Beyond the gate that once rang with your music,
That signaled celebration in your return,
And now sings only songs of wind and emptiness?
And what adventure can I find without you,
Free at last when I no longer long for freedom?
How has your once familiar face grown older,
When in my mirror I see just a stranger?
If I would meet you on a street in summer
How would you greet me if you even knew me?
Perhaps you have been gone too long to wonder
Or remember how we spent our time together.
Perhaps you would not know me if you saw me
And have forgotten even how to find me.
The road beyond the gate does not invite me.
Some are made for seeking, others finding.
I glance out past the trees and garden,
Listen for the gate to close behind you,
Hear your footsteps and your soft voice singing.

Margaret Dinzler Shaw

The No-Net World

The No-Net World

Deep in your heart, you always believed
There was a barrier, a secret shield
Keeping you safe from the street
Secretly, you knew
Your good shoes and your warm lined gloves
Kept you apart, and safe
From the man with the cup in his hand
and the boy with the cardboard sign
and the woman with the bloated legs
and the girl with the begging eyes
From the weathered women railing at God
And the shadows at the ashcan fires
From the need to ask, no choices left:
Mister, can you please . . . ?

What did you, from the cushioned world
Of buffers, alternatives, other ways to turn
Of loans from family friends
Of credit cards and healthy children
Of grocers who smiled because they knew how well you ate:
What did you have in common
With the concrete world of need?
Secretly, you knew, so surely you believed
You could never fall so low

Welcome to the no-net world.

Then I got fired one day
I got fired one day
Lost my job and then my house
I got fired one day.

Now your debts mount up like garbage
And a layoff's coming soon
And you have to see a doctor and insurance just pays half
And your folks who lent you money
Just can't help you anymore
And the loans are coming due; still, the force field is there,
In the lining of the gloves, in the good if now used shoes
You will never stand like that goddamned bum
Holding the door at the bank too tired to whore or steal
Saying please ma'am, please ma'am please . . .

Then I got HIV
I got HIV
They found out
I lost my job
I got HIV

Welcome to the no-net world

You would never see hunger on the face of your child
When she came home from school there would always be
Apples and rice and chicken and beans
Milk and carrots and peas
Now there's two days left till payday
And just one last can of corn and she's home, laughing
Hungry, hi, I'm home, ma, what's for lunch

Welcome to the no-net world

Are you hungry? Good: Ready, set, line up, let's go:
You can get on line on Monday
for the lunch meal that's on Tuesday
and the shelter line's for Thursday
but you have to sign up Monday
But you stayed there just last Wednesday
so you can't come back till Friday

And the food stamps place is downtown
And the welfare place is uptown
And the Medicaid is westside
And the hospital is eastside
No I can't give you a token
No I can't give you a token
No I can't give you a token
Don't you know you'll only drink?

Hell, yes.

Like a child praying to God
You believed in forever
you thought home and hearth were,
Not for everyone of course,
But surely for you:

Only in the nightmares
Rare unremembered dreams
Did you stand by the door of the bank
Saying
Yes ma'am, God bless you ma'am
Please.

Don't get sick
Don't let anyone you love get sick
Don't be mentally ill
Don't lose your job
Don't be without money for a second
Don't make any mistakes

Welcome to the no-net world

Larissa Shmailo

Yesterday

Yesterday, all my troubles seemed so far away.
Now it looks as though they're here to stay.
Oh, I believe in yesterday.

I believe in yesterday. Yesterday was syphilis and gonorrhea.
A shot of penicillin was the panacea.
My unwanted pregnancy did not mean the death of me.
It all turned out okay, yesterday.
Nothing will ever be the same
since HIV's been linked to my name.
My pretty black skin with the cheeks a dark pink
has been destroyed by festering sores that burst and stink.
When did HIV become a sister's scourge?
Friends and family abandon me, and I lose courage.
Sisters in Africa perish in large numbers while America
turns its back and slumbers. My sisters cry out
to the super nations to end their degradation: Send in
the AIDS cocktail along with clean water. Help wipe out
both AIDS and cholera. Hollah! Why is it money or my life?
Why don't you care just because I'm not your wife?
You erase my black face, slow your pace in the race for a cure.
How much more suffering must my sisters endure?
Who knew my progress would cause you such distress?
When I stopped being mammy, you decided to abandon me.
When I became the boss, you built me a cross.
You think immigrants make better maids
so what does it matter that I got AIDS?

Yesterday, all America's troubles seemed so far away.
Now it looks as though they're here to stay.
Oh, America believed in yesterday.

I think it finally found a way to bring back yesterday.

Sista Girl (Rev. Gail Haliburton)

Long Island Just Isn't Long Enough

They call it Long Island, but
it's just not long enough to
keep moving to where there
are no black people, no yellow people, no brown people,
speaking in two languages, living in two Americas,
blending two cultures.
Rikers is a gated community, but
i wouldn't want to live there.
Rikers and Hempstead have the same racial composition.
i escaped here, merely finding my carefully planned, secretly
executed tunnel led to the prison cafeteria instead of outside
of broken dreams.
And you sold the house in Brooklyn for this?
And you left your country for this?
And you spent your life's savings for this?
The schools still suck
and now there's no one to babysit Ayesha.
Wasn't it they who taught you
taxation without representation just isn't fair?
He says, "Everywhere we move, white people move away."
I ask him, "Why?"
He says, "They don't like us."
Everywhere i move, white people move away
like lemmings to the Long Island Sound.
i am close on your heels,
first walk, then run, now swim
because Long Island just isn't long enough
since you can't have no ark without me
you can't have an ark without me.

Marcia McNair

Hope Clutches, Time Waits

Hope clutches at disaster
painting pretty pictures
then fades into stretched photos
always wanting, sometimes lost

drenched in failure
it sulks
ashamed of a reality
it never should have known

back again and again
it knows its name
and where to stay
disguised as an innocent

Time waits with pen in hand
solid at the door
watching our cool
collective conscience

waits for me to think
of small important things
then laughs
and writes in blood

E. Willa Haas

Home Front, 1945

She only used half her sugar rations,
gave up her girdle, hairpins, silks, Jergens Lotion,
stood when Kate Smith boomed on the radio
"God Bless America," penciled brown seams
on bare legs, wore Victory Red Lipstick
to kiss Iwo Jima on the map, hoed
her Victory Plot, picked off aphids, thrips,
slugs, leafhoppers, made a Hitler scarecrow,
tossed Mildred Pierce Victory Salad
with hated pot cheese, noodles, tuna, beans,
to waive her meat rations, and never had
even a taste of Swann's Down Cake. *Oh, please,*
 my jitterbugging, lindy-hopping marine,
 my Yankee fan, Yankee man, come home to me.

Rochelle Jewel Shapiro

Shalimar

First perfume for the country girl
Christmas joy from the New Jersey boy
arriving in his shiny Impala to win
the heart of my big sister.

Whiffs of that deep aroma evoke memories still
of my blue velvet dress and the cool stiff feel
of cadet gray as sensuous strains of
"My Funny Valentine" float through stone
arches into Hudson Valley air.

How my sixteen-year-old heart would quicken
as I rounded the cliff-high curves
of Storm King Mountain and entered
the testosterone world that was West Point.

How many of those proud young men
were wasted in the killing fields
while my life grew from naive
young girl in the blue velvet dress
to the woman who knows
how wretched are these wars of men.

Beda Lyon

How Many Wars

First you were a boy,
Then you were a man,
Later still a soldier taking orders.
Now you are a wound
With a woeful past,
Lying in a room with many others.
Now you are the pain
That mocks you as you think
Of blood and noise and fears unbearable.
You fear not for yourself
Or what is yet to come,
But dead yet open eyes, their look so terrible.
First you were a boy,
Then you were a man,
Later still a soldier taught to kill.
Now you are a bandage
With a soul inside,
Waiting for the shattered world to heal.

Sharon Bourke

War Wounds

Send in the soldiers
to witness
the vacant eyes
the soiled souls
the rivers of pain
crisscrossing the
frail bodies of
the young and the old

Who will heal
the festering wounds
or peel the crusted
life blood
off the newly-minted
patriot
yet, no longer one?

Ines Senna Shaw

Sewing the Bullet Holes

When I finally could sew his damage clothes,
I looked at the small hole in his heavy coat
then tossed it aside — amazed.
I decided to leave it that way, for luck.
The course threads of his burgundy sweater
seemed to reknit after the slug pushed through.
The shirt was creased and bloody, not torn,
so it must have been crumpled above his waist.

But the slacks required attention.
The bullet entered near the back seam of the waistband
and lodged under the skin at the base of the spine.
A cop pulled it out like a splinter
of shrapnel.
The doctors called it a miracle.

They were gray corduroy, worn soft.
The fiber in the back of the band was shredded
and a small tuft of wine-colored wool
was embedded in a dent in the stiff white buckram.
He wore no belt that day,
so merely the thickness of buckram
shifted the bullet's angle of entry
downward to a fabric more vulnerable
and kept the bullet near the surface of his flesh.

The white cotton nearest his body was stained.
My finger probed the hole and followed the route
over and over. The way I kept asking what happened
after they held the gun to your head?
What did you do?
What did they say?
What did you think?

Finally I threaded the needle
and stitched the gap closed.

It took longer for the scab to heal.
Now a shiny spot marks the wound, a glossy scar.
Now when he lies on me
and my hands reach around his back to press
his bulk against my crest,
I find the point of entry and gently rub.

My fingers search his flesh, feel the bullet,
then with a shudder
they pull it out.

Patti Tana

Seven Days

Seven days ago, after the storm,
Over dazzling white drifts, under a sapphire sky,
Our skis and polls in tandem, together we two.

Seven nights later, after the storm,
Beneath white sheets, in the ebbing twilight,
Too sudden, too warm, too still, alone you lie.

The Curtain

On the other side of the curtain,
An elderly woman bids goodbye and packs for home;
Obscene chatter of today's lunches and tomorrow's weather.

On our side of the curtain,
We too bid goodbye,
Our lives suspended between numbness and pain.

The Dining Room Clock

I dreamed last night that the dining room clock had stopped.
The key in your hand always wound its spring.
Your energy made our hours sing.

Bernadine Brown

Cartographer of the Breast

After the doctor saw the lump, a white bulb
in the gray moon of my mammogram,
the weeks, the wait in the clinic flipping
through *Newsweek,*
the needle, the star-like scar
turned in slow motion.

I floated into zero gravity,
my breast sampled for alien elements,
results sorted under Latin names
filed away in the belly of a computer.

Mother, nipple-less after the mastectomy,
father gently stroke-skimming
the air above the the scar
to let her know he sees the flesh
that was, that fed their babies,
less perfect now,
but printed with memory.

She stays silent.
With craters so wide,
how to test the safe grounds
of conversation?

What can we say
about our role in the doctor's mission
but carry the line
where the scalpel met the flesh?

And seas later
— unlike the pain of birthing
where relief sings in your limbs —

we hope our feet meet earth.

Pramila Venkateswaran

Because

Because a puppy is *now!* while the news
is grief for yesterday and fear
for tomorrow, we drive to the animal shelter
the Sunday after the Towers collapse.
The shelter is packed with children
eager to make a dog wag its tail
or be licked by a cat's sandpaper tongue.
Parents who had said no or when you're older
are eager to give their kids something
to watch besides the rising toll.

I'd heard the news in the car as I drove home
from my second radiation treatment
and it seemed unreal at first, unreal
as the news in August when a smiley-face
computer voice announced, "You've got cancer!"
— unreal until the surgeon cut
the nodule from my breast and I could feel
the tender reality. It's small, he said,
a pea or a pearl, or a nuclear reactor I thought
and where else are they lurking, these ticking bombs?

September explosions and the thousands dead
make the threat inside my body seem smaller,
so we stop in front of a sleepy chocolate pointer
with white patches on her face and chest
and the tip of her tail. Careful for the stitches
in her belly, we place her on the table where she
shakes off sleep and invites us to fall in love.
Before we walk out with her in my arms, a sign
warns, "Are you ready for a fifteen-year commitment?"
and I say sure, I'll take it — give me fifteen years.

Patti Tana

Ground Zero, Ajar

I saw a river of crimson blood
run over the porous body
of the earth
saturated underneath
with torment
and fragments of life

I heard hearts beating
in the rhythm of tomorrow
until the murderers' desire
to obliterate
exploded and nothing was left
but dust devils swirling in the air . . .

Ines Senna Shaw

Sacred Space

Sacred Space

the muse chants
earth, wind, fire, air
crystals, old photos, candles
wait on an antique bookcase

the ritual begins
come forth, come forth
daughters of the moon
circle of the wise

a white candle burns
slender rod dipped in anointed beeswax
a ripe red pomegranate — cut open
with the sacred knife

the flame dances on the night-draped wall
maternal mentors appear
for a moment
eternity holds her hand

Johanna Mastrototaro

No Moon

No moon
just your bare feet
one rubbing another
a bead of sweat
strung between your breasts
darkening planets
in the cotton hollow
beneath your arms.

Night puts its thick lips
to our foreheads
plants the kiss
then leaves us to our kitchen
where we click our tongues
and shake our grins
at this shuttered town
that has locked its doors
left its stray men
to beat their wings
like moths
beneath its lamps
and pray us to sleep
for the night.

It is best
that this town
dreams behind its screens
that the men
stay out
because we do not sleep
and we cannot be followed.

Cicadas like castanets
pull us to our feet
press us hip to hip
not to each other
but to why we meet.
We have come
to make our mothers
leave their forests
sweep their hems
across overgrown paths
until their eyes wink
in the small sightings we have
of dark bodies that have taken flight.

And then
and then
when we are
so
close
to finding what we
miss not having had
so close
to becoming shadows
within the shadows
of what we do not
understand
but witness together
a phantom hand
shakes us into chatter
like tambourines.

I will see
gypsy fires flicker
in the dark green
of your eyes
your lips
press their tongue
for water.
Only then
will I feel the heat
the need for sleep
only then
will I be ready
for good night
and the way you reach
the small clearing
at the base of my spine
to pull me to you
in this womanloss
this womanlove
that needs no moon
to find its way.

Linda Opyr

Sister Shaman

say your magic words
take us to another time
remind me of when we took for granted
the presence of each other
when we traveled through a river
of school, five & dime stores, movie theaters, boys
say the names of long ago places
I can enter in spiritual shoes
unravel your stories like soft silk
spin your spell as we sit together
over the warmth of coffee
in your company I am always young
waiting for you after school when
we hold hands to cross a street
to the other side

Paula Camacho

The Inn of Neruda in Santiago

On place mats brown and smooth
as butcher paper, italicized words,
Pablo Neruda's *Oda al Pan*, a flow
of poetry in praise of bread
its need for fire and water
to create roundness,
flavor, denseness,
life-affirming beauty

It is International Women's Day
my Chilean "daughter"
her daughters and I are each
given a red rose and serenaded
with sad songs, love songs,
gay songs, songs
in praise of women's roundness,
beauty, deeds, struggles,
our life-nurturing bodies

The atmosphere envelops me,
the music, the camaraderie
Soothed, thrilled
by what my eyes see
what my ears hear
certain that images of this
moment will tiptoe into my
heart's mind, bring back
a night when women and
bread were celebrated
at the Inn of Neruda

Beatrice G. Davis

Respite

Dear bread out of the pan,
Windowful of starlight,
Hour
Gathered like a shared blanket
Around our shoulders,
Rare peace before rare dawn,
We sit, speaking softly
Before setting out.

Sharon Bourke

Pie Heaven

God is still in the kitchen,
has just wiped the last few flakes
of dough from the counter
and now dries both hands
on the apron's white cotton,
satisfied.

The window is open with
afternoon, the color of butter.
A beam of sun reaches
for the red-checked cloth
that tops the pie
that waits on the sill.

God looks up,
sees the coarsest pair
of hands lift that pie
down the bent-grass path
that leads to the tracks
where trains whistle away the darkness.

God watches every time, notices
the trees, their peaches —
some that will ripen, be picked,
those that the wind will shake
into storm.

This is pie heaven.
Nothing is ready-made,
low carb or sugar free.
The weight of the world
not yet crimping God's style.

Linda Opyr

Overnight Guest

We sat at breakfast, speaking of the moon
And how it showed itself the night before
Then hid
As clouds swept past its lustrous face
Telling their ancient stories
(Light and dark,
Arrivals, departures)
Then silent, we pondered
How dreams from which we just awoke
Were outshone
Flooded by the brilliance of the night before
Its messages long lingering
(A lifting, a falling,
A birth, a death)
Dear Moon
Serene
Still singing as you go
Your clouds in tow
Still crying "Oh"

Sharon Bourke

Consider the Constellations

consider the constellations
huntress's bow chariots churning
hurtling burning spinning lost
like cities undersea
stars spill across the sky

through winter sun the world blazes
in tough brilliance
blossoms hold tight to themselves
like babies' fists
a despot might call it insolence

I must remember to praise sunrise
must look inside the commotion
the jumble the jigsaw the jewelweed
to stumble to trod on to live to love
the leaf my face the sun

ah world perfectly formed oak gall
prickly obdurate world infinite in brown
at dawn as it settles like a comeliness
a shawl oh knotted skein
oh clotted world convergent world   us   all!

Ellen Rittberg

Pieta

Water surrounds them in the deep wood tub.

Her mother's arms cradle her head and knees,
steam rises from the dark pool of water
caressing with the reverence of ancestors.

Outside the window, snow.
A mist of ice gathers in the wind
blowing onto the sills.

Above their heads a brass oil lamp washes
faces in light, the daughter's young skin
a watery petal, her hair carefully gathered.

They float together, a mother giving
her grown daughter a bath.
The young woman, deformed from mercury,
flows motionless in her arms.

The radiance of their faces, the sacrament
of warm water and weightlessness,
how they smile at each other
engrave my memory.

*Ryoko Uemura, the mother, suggested the bathing chamber
for W. Eugene Smith's photograph of mercury poisoning
victims in Minamata, Japan: "Tomoko and Mother in the Bath"*

Gladys Henderson

The Holiest Blessing

Either an infant or a child, the young or very old,
Either a helpless one or brave, either the weak or very bold,
Either a villain or the righteous or someone in between,
The restless or the calm, anxious or serene,
Either the wise one or the fool, the kind one or the cruel,
The one who was loved and cared, was cautious or dared,
The one who was scolded or the one who scolds,
The poorest of them all or the one with silver and gold —
When all are in great need, their last wish,
Every one and all,
One name, one name only, "Mother" is the name they call.

When they are down and crushed with pain,
When their phantom pain returns again and again,
When their bodies are taken
By burning fever or chilling cold,
More so when they know the end is near or they are told
That no healing hand can heal them any more,
That there is no room to bargain
Or finish the leftover chore,
That they can't buy time even with money and gold —
Just before they surrender their body and their soul
Their cloudy eyes search for the eternal peaceful goal.
Some cry, some laugh, some beg and cajole,
Their eyes move up and down and they roll around
Just before they go into the fetal position and fold
Their trembling arms reach for Her before turning cold.

Screaming or pleading with tearful eyes,
They don't care any more if they look foolish or wise,
They ask for the marker and the board
And write "Mother" or whisper the word
Just before they leave the temporary world.
It seems all the mothers do come in the end, I'm told
All carry a torch above the faces they hold.
That is why a dying infant or child, the young and the old
All have translucent face and faint smile
With their last words:
"Help me, Mama, hold my hand and help me cross the road,
Kiss me one more time and hold me tight,
Mama, just hold!"

Narges Rothermel

Emily Dickinson to Her Visitors

My tombstone says I was "called back" —
though perhaps I was not alive
in house or town of ache and lack —
what others could not hear, I did.

I learned to breathe a joy
of sound — yet it too was
taken, riven, and destroyed
by those who followed marching tunes.

I became — long before entombed —
the song that moves night skies, the tides
and sparrow's wings. On that ride
I disappeared — and never died.

Sally Ann Drucker

Grandmother's Veins

Grandmother's Veins

I used to watch them trace her skin
graceful and familiar and mysterious as
the ceiling cracks I traveled as I lay in bed
a map I learned to read
before I learned to read;
they showed the way.

The first time they appeared on me
I was amazed to see the tiny asterisk
a pale reminder of what flows
so close beneath the surface: my blood,
her blood, the blood that circles down
the mountains of the generations.

Now purple rivulets run wild
across my ankle bone, behind my knee
pale trickles underneath my eyes.

My skin grows tough as it grows thin.
My freckles spread; age spots begin.
I stroke my arm as I stroked hers
to touch the marks of birth, of death
admiring the marbled wrapping
of gifts given, gifts received.

Susan Astor

Passages: First Visit to Vermont

The shady places are still frozen
the sunny spots have turned to mud.
The new large wheel stroller handles
the unpaved road well enough that you rest
your lashes on your apple cheeks
and settle within your fleece cocoon.

The cloudless sky is fringed with piney points
and I am glad to be a part of such a day.

Are you dreaming, Little One, of your first
horse encounter or a striped cat sprinting
from the barn to rub his side on human leg?
Are your dreams full of adoring
faces drinking in your every move?

When eyes open at walk's end will you
recognize me as the one who wants remembering
for your lifetime, as I remember a sweet
sweaty bosom wrapped in apron,
hand slipping quarters into my pocket,
gnarled hand reaching up to pat blond curls?

Beda Lyon

Grandmothers

They stand in the doorway
between the crayon world
and the shadow world,
belonging to neither.
They exist only in the doorway.

They teach the children
what letters are,
how they grow into words
and words into sentences.
They lead the children
into the world that words make.

They are the signposts, the guides
to keep the children safe.
But eventually they must lead them
to the edge,
the absence of words.
They are the first teachers
of loss

Barbara Lucas

Double Nickels I

Time was when a woman could
sit a bit and reflect
while she slowly transformed
into a wise old sage
with grandkids rollicking
around her plump feet,
her stories creating a link in the chain
of gentle memories.

Time was when she could savor
her accumulated wisdom
and keep her secrets,
quietly smiling into the shadows
of remembered winter nights
and warm summer days,
the crunch of fall,
the drizzle of spring.
Life rolled on her tongue,
settled into her heart
and let her breathe.

Time was when her soul flew free,
soared to the sky,
floated to earth
and settled into the gentle
rocking of the waves.
Time was when she could
sit a bit and understand
that her seasons pass with
the color of the leaves,
the snow and the rain nourish her
and she brings forth flowers
that bloom into eternity.

Lynn Green

Double Nickels II

But hold on — here comes granny
stuck to her cell phone
sporting two-inch spikes
with hair of many hues
off to the gym to keep that old
(did I say old — heaven forbid)
ticker going beyond any natural lifetime.

We're gals out to have fun,
to show the world that we still
got what it takes
(despite our backs, knees, and tennis elbows)
that we can keep up with the best
(damn our stomachs, livers, and bladders)
and that we're standing on the neck
of old Father Time
cutting off his air with our $100 Reeboks.

Lynn Green

No Replacement

I am the last
of my generation
who spans the gap
between English and
an old Sicilian dialect

the translator
of telephone calls
a mediator for questions
a decipherer
for visiting relatives

no offspring or cousin
to connect
no voice that travels
from vast spaces
to spaces in the heart

Maria Manobianco

Preparations

Standing in ordered suburbs,
I chop the walnuts
In my Cuisinart.
Tossing back a brown lock of curl
My thoughts are visited
By ancient sisters

    Who stood in ghettos in wild Russia
    With sepia waves draping one eye
    Preparing their walnuts and hoping
    Their children would grow to love

        The sweet wine, nuts, apples
        And the certain balance
        Of the bitter herbs.

Marcia Silverberg Pulewitz

Grandmother's Bedside

Come closer. Let me see those earrings.
Nice. You said your mother-in-law gave
them to you? She has good taste.
Sit comfortably on my bed. I don't
let anyone sit so close to grandma.
These bangles are heavy. Good to know
those jewelers haven't cheated.
Got to watch out, or those wretches
will sneak more copper into the gold.

I like how you painted me in blue silk,
hint of gold against my collarbone.
Makes me look taller than I am, masking
the 80 years bending me as if in revenge
for twisting to my will that trickster
fate that drives widows like me to choose
poverty or death. Anyway, enough about me.
Your mother, does she have the same maid,
the one with the crooked teeth?

And that cook, I heard you sent her away.
Good. Only connoisseurs know
the extraordinary. I'd rather cook
my own meal suited to my taste
than put up with shit that passes for food.

Pramila Venkateswaran

Birds & Green Ribbons Flying

My granddaughter asks me to write out my life.
Knowing I love the freedom of birds, she brings me
A journal covered with birds and green ribbons flying.

How far back should I go?
All of it, Granma, says this daughter of my son.
It will help me.
She is the soft side of my insides.

I play up the mistakes to show her how I learned
To get through, dry my tears to make it all fit.
Her blue eyes shine like my deep brown eyes once did.

What here in this poor life will teach her to be
Bold and self-loving
To blow the fear away.

How can I tell her about the small voice, deep and low
Saying: eighty-one
Reminding me of this unbelievable age.

That with all of my love for her I cannot stay forever,
And that going, I know I will not see her ever again
Or even be able to think of her.

Instead I tell her how to choose a man,
How to make it work, and surely to love her work.
That independence alone can be brittle.
We cannot saw off dependent needs like an old tree stump.

But Granma, what is most important?
Smoothing her long shining hair, I make her giggle
As I tickle the back of her neck.

E. Willa Haas

The Cranes

I had a stone in my pocket,
carrying it with me for weeks

finding that throughout the day
my hand would return to my side

my thumb upon the small, cool
hollow until it grew warm.

And I'd be thinking of something
I could not name, just beyond me

something grey, melancholy
as a winter beach, something caught

below brushbound fallen leaves
a long ago journey on a footless path.

Nana died today, you said.
It's ok . . . she'd stopped eating

and wasn't talking, but, you know,
she raised us . . . and she was my Nana.

As you spoke, my hand slipped
inside its pocket, found its stone.

And I remembered the cranes
their steps ⸺ long-legged, sure

until the question marks of their bodies
fold in upon themselves and

sleek white sails fill the sky

Linda Opyr

I Ate My Mother's Hair

I Ate My Mother's Hair

& I'd like to think some remnants
of those fine white tresses remain

in me still. I didn't ingest her hair
on purpose, standing behind her

as she sat on a stool in the shower
stall of her nursing home bathroom,

tile floor catching snippets I cut
from her statue-still head. What

could I do with the comb when
I had to wield the scissors with one

hand, clasp her locks with the other —
mother's tangled brain not letting her

grasp that she could ease my task,
she could turn her head when asked

hold the comb & look in the mirror
when I finished, see what a fine job I did?

Month after month, for seven years,
I stood at the sink in that nursing home

bathroom, rinsed her silvery traces out
of my mouth, sadness washing over me.

Ruth Sabath Rosenthal

What I Couldn't Swallow

sticks in my throat
like the ragged claw
of a sea urchin —

my mother's blame
my father's rage —
I should have been braver
I should have been smarter
I should have been a boy
or a woman without a tongue

what I couldn't swallow
sticks in my throat
like the ragged claw
of a sea urchin —

your hate
like purple seaweed
darkening the blue of your eyes
your vice like my mother's
echoing from the large shell
I crouch in, arms folded
knees to my chin
swallowing the sea
in long, steady gulps

Gloria g. Murray

Upon Hearing Her Sing

I forgot
the way bile stuck — a hard pit
in the swell of her throat
how she lay on the couch, a cold towel
pressed over pulsing temples
the way she screeched in a pitch
that flew over the wall like a home run

how she carried her gloom in a covered
dish to the dinner table every evening
how she limped on a swollen leg
wrapped in support hose, flowers
on her house dress pale
from so many washings

I forgot
until I heard her soprano voice
as if from the throat of a bird
freed from its cage, wings teetering
in flight, albatross body suddenly
smashing against the closed windows

Gloria g. Murray

My Mother's Fruitbowl

swells like an over ripe melon.
It sits with enormous knees
and shoulders
at the center of the table,
and I am to pick an offering
from this fragrant, bulbous monster.

It is a ritual that permits us
to engage in conversation.

There are brown speckled bananas
turning to nectar in their skins;
apples rusting from within
flattened where they rest against the
glass.

Have a plum, and she tosses me
something swollen and tender,
silky to its membrane,
the color of a bruise.

Whatever remains for my visits
is all sugar, or tart:
grapes that pucker at the
puncture mark,
peaches too proud, too hard
and dry to ooze.

She teaches me. I may have grown
beyond her sugared milk,
but I will taste her fruit.

Mindy Kronenberg

Those Saturday Nights

I never had enough of holding you.
You cared for me with an efficient hand.
But on those nights you gave me a shampoo,
then pressed my face against your breast, I'd stand
as in a trance and spellbound while you dried
my hair. I never wanted it to end,
for only then was I allowed inside
your arms, to feel your body warm, and blend
myself into your mother-smell, my old
remembered ecstasy. Otherwise,
you handled me, but never could you hold.
Now you are old, and I am in a vise.
Now death is near, you clutch me and implore.
Now I am held, who was not held before.

Gail Chapman

Astronomy Lesson

It was so far away, you said, and light
would take so long to travel that we could
be looking at the distant past. The sight
of Jesus on the cross, conversely, would
be seen if we were gazing from some star.
I shivered in the cold November night.
Or someone may be watching from afar,
you said, and see the winter chill turn white
the vapor of our breath, and wonder who
this long-dead father and his child had been,
with white snow falling, made immortal through
the shaft of streetlight they were standing in,
transported from their finite time and place
to move forever through the dark of space.

Gail Chapman

Silently and Ceaselessly

They're on their honeymoon now,
      on the shoreline of a lake's early spring,
    gently rippling as a dream that inspires
      such ruddiness in their cheeks, a rosy solace
        in their outlooks as they look off
          past the frame of their rowboat
  in which their legs so intertwine,
it's as if they've only three between them,
    and they're so young, young enough to be my children,
      as they sit at the prow, balanced on mere promise,
    listening to the songs of this lake
      that are for their ears only,
        as silently and ceaselessly these songs
would come to nourish the seeds their bodies believed in
  and they hold each other around their necks,
    their heads touching, their hair intertwined,
so thick, dark, and raised with waves,
      redolent of the rippling that would carry them
        to the distant side of the lake,
      despite the efforts of their oars,
  disarmed by trust and sickness,
by anger, loneliness, and fear,
  but mostly, they would be disarmed by love,
    a gently, rippling, limitless discovery,
    and here where more than one thin nail
    keeps them from the gravity of time,
      beyond the wormhole-eaten corner
they can't see through,
      as Big Bros. carts off their crystal bowls,
      they're on their honeymoon now.

Hilda and Rudy Leibowitz   Lakewood, New Jersey, 1941

Gayl Teller

My Mother, the Swimmer

My mother, the swim counselor,
is telling me again about her crawl —
the width of its arcs, her sure flutter
kick, how polished. And how stranded
seven flights above Lexington all
summer, she thinks it's only right
that I drive her to Jones Beach
so she can see the ocean —
this one small pleasure.

So she can dream back, I think,
the pleasure of the body, cutting
a swath, plying whatever blue
seam and current the ocean
opens for her, arms synchronous and keeping
half-time with her legs, thrumming,
shattering the surface that recomposes
itself, even as it's broken.

The ocean is in perfect form
for my mother, unraveling
its blue scrolls, and she reminds me
how we swam at Amagansett
in wild water like this —
foolhardy, the two of us alone
except for some kids with wet suits
and boards. And do I remember
that strange man who walked up to marvel
at her, a woman of her age
braving it?

Now she stands in the shallows
to the shins, hands clasped behind her
in the stance of the watcher, remembering
the day that made her afraid:
the tow overwhelming her
stroke and foothold.

And she pleads with me
not to risk it. One day, she says,
I'll stand in her place, maybe
my daughter among the swimmers, maybe
remembering her. And wouldn't
I like the bronze medal she won
for the crawl, the one
she uses for a paperweight now —
memento of my mother,
the swimmer? Wouldn't I like
to remember her whole?

Kathrine Jason

Return of My Father

Last night you came back to me where I stood
in the kitchen — of all places — wearing the guise
of domesticity and middle age. Did I summon you

there as I practiced your example, scouring
the sink's homely, pitted porcelain until
my arm ached with the effort you always urged —

"elbow grease." Leaning into it I became
in that moment my father's daughter, and I turned
towards my inkling of you, towards your praise.

I might have spoken out loud to put you
at ease, maybe I even lifted my hands
from the blue Ajax grease to lead you upstairs.

But mounting the landing, when I turned
to show you my one perfect work, now eight,
sleeping behind her perfect scrim

of sleep, I stood alone with my epiphany
and my hands dripping blue
on the floor of her room. What could I do but

return to my task, thinking you would find it
still unpolished and that we would laugh together
at how unchanged I am, in my life's dead center.

Kathrine Jason

Defying Gravity

My mother struggles to rise from her chair,
wrestling with dignity
to stand on her own.
Earth draws her near, holds fast.

When I reach out
she waves me away,
wants to do it herself
the way she has for ninety-six years.

The day the Pope died, a great white oak
snapped in my yard
before a strong gust of wind,
fell across the bridge and into the pond.

Between birth and dead is a sweet freedom
to live beyond regret, beyond despair.

Patti Tana

A Small Voice

A Small Voice

Today my heart hurts —
the familiar ache began yesterday
an ordinary summer day
as I sat on the beach
a little girl near me stood shivering
as her mother wrapped her
safely in a pink and white striped beach towel
carefully the mother removed the wet, sandy bathing suit
from the twisting, turning little body
naked the little one hovered close to the mother
hiding herself in the familiar embrace
the mother sprinkled baby powder generously
over the child
a cloud of white smoothed away the sticky, sandy beach
the little girl stepped into the white cotton panties
her mother held hidden under the towel
then she rested in her mother's lap

as the wind blew a whiff of powder in my direction
a small voice within me cried out

Johanna Mastrototaro

To the Woman Who Gave Me
My Sunrise

I sit on the plane
and I think of you

Now she is mine
because she was yours

You will want
I will have
You will long
and I will be full
Your child is now
my child
Your yesterday
is now my tomorrow

I look forward out the window
at the rising sun
and our child turns
to see the sun setting
in China

Mary Gund

Circular Motion

for my father

The love we always had is based in the round —
the warm grasp of your hand in mine
as we made our way to the playground,
the circular motion of the swing
as you wildly pushed me against
the will of the earth.

My lenses curve to the same cock-eyed
rhythm as yours, and our teeth
bend toward each other
with the same mad crunch.

Before I was born, you and mom
would whirl through our tiny flat
to modern music, eyes closed
in an ecstasy that could prove
godly or dangerous.
I picked up the song in my blood,
embraced the old records on
our monograph player and tossed
myself around the room
in the same fierce spirit.

Together we watched cowboys on TV
raise lassos high over their heads,
and you taught me how to ball my fist
against the angular threat of anyone.

Most of all, I remember
the wheels of my bike spinning
as you ran alongside me until
your hands allowed a curve of space
to cushion the bar — and let go.
Your shouts became smaller and smaller,
the words bouncing back to me
through the years:
you can do it   you can do it

Mindy Kronenberg

Self-Portrait

Palest blue, our twin crescent eyepools
rimmed by ghostly fringe. My hair, like his too —
brown flecked with gray, wooly, easily frizzed.
His broad forehead and rounded-cliff cheekbones
also appear in my mirror. I can't see
myself without him. I cannot let him be,
nor he, me. He seeps into my poetry
like spilled tea,
a sugar cube held between his teeth.

All day I speak to the dead. How can it be
that now I'm only three years
from the age my father was
when he died? "Look, Daddy, I can tap dance."
Hop, brush, brush, step-step.
Zol zein shtil! you bellowed.

Now your prize fighter fists stay clasped
on the unbreathing barrel of your chest,
but your blows still break
the crest of my dreams.
Zol zein shtil!

Rochelle Jewel Shapiro

Simulacrum

My daughter had a world
in miniature, caught
inside a dome of glass.
Strange weather there,
it snowed and snowed,
white spells drifting down
over the house
with its bare tree alongside,
a few stars overhead
and three tidy figures
that stood for us.   Or so

I understood when it slipped
from her hand, shattering —
a whole world lost
for which she cried and cried.

Childhood is like that too,
first all-encompassing, holding
us in as if without end. Of mine
I own some cold token
that fits in one hand.

Kathrine Jason

Backpack Girl

May she linger like this unhurried
    by have-tos as she sits and stirs
        her song into swimming colors

shocked with shells and leaves laced
    with sand and floating bits of seaweed
        ladling her bucket by the sea with foam

from waves and myriads of miniscule
    living ingredients like little motors
        with which a little girl generates

such apple-pizza goodness — "Taste!"
    we all want what she scoops out
        upon a sieve for each of us

dripping them nameless and unseen
    into gobbling sand beneath our feet
        as leaving-time reminds it's time

she pulls with each strap onto each shoulder
    gladly rushing into the feel of the clasp
        of her already agenda-seeking backpack.

Gayl Teller

Wading the Tidal Pools

He climbs to his feet, startled from the narrow bench
where he sat all morning watching. He shades the sun
from his eyes and with a hand cupped round his mouth,
my father calls my name and gestures that I should come.

Morning has given way to his cries. I leave behind tidal
pools filled with blameless creatures I have baptized,
giving them names, smoothing their perfect bodies
with my fingers, watching sadly as they escape
the imperfect prison of my cupped palms.

Over his alarms and across the black rocks I scurry,
making my way back to him. Above the horizon
the sun pours crimson, my hair and face on fire.
A child's tee shirt covers newly-formed breasts.

Men have begun to walk down the hill toward
their boats and have stopped to admire what has emerged
at the water's edge. My father measures their closeness
to me by the lines of the falling tide, but nothing
will stop its flowing.

Gladys Henderson

Rosebuds

1988

I see my daughter's breasts
And avert my eyes:
I am her mother and should not stare.

But, oh,
That almost indiscernible feeling
That waves through my body at their sight.
Not arousal, not sexual excitement.
No, something more like a familiar memory. . .
Like the memory of standing in wide open spaces.

Rosebuds
Softening the nipples
No longer specific marks on a map
Showing exact location
Now
Ever so slightly raised, and opening,
Puffy and soft, like eyes that have cried,
Cartographic hints
Of trends and readiness for growth.

Nine years old,
Already not a little girl . . .
Lines lengthened
Face, no longer cute — pretty.

With urgency born in her body
She, indeed, begins
To view her self as woman.

Andrea Kaufman

Blood Sisters

"Don't touch,"
she'd call
from the edge of the bed
where she sat
putting on the stocking
she had rolled into her hands,
or letting the straps of a slip
fall to her shoulders.

"I won't," I'd answer,
"I'm just looking."
But of course I was really
just lurking
there at the beveled edges
of my mother's perfume tray.
She'd pull the dress
over her head,
step into her shoes
and then come to the mirror
above the tray.

She'd look up,
the oh of her lips
ready to be painted,
her cheeks glowing
beneath the small brush.
And then the moment
I'd waited for.

She'd lift a bottle
then its cap
and with two fingers
touch the perfume

to her neck, wrists.
I knew the choices —
pink cap — Ambush
black label — Tabu
White Shoulders
Faberge —
but not the choice.

"How do you know
which one to use?"
I'd ask.
"You just know —
you'll see.

When you get older."
At that
she'd tug me away
from the bits of us
reflected in the bits of tray
beneath the carefully angled bottles.

But if I were lucky
and she not too rushed,
she'd dab those same two fingers
to my small wrists,
the two of us blood sisters
in our when-the-time-comes
knowing
secret
without my having
to touch
a thing.

Linda Opyr

Paper Children

My mother often spoke
of her life in another land
and of an aunt
who would hold pictures
in her hand
and tearfully say
"These are my children
my paper children
they live an ocean away."

I listened
but did not hear
the meaning of
those anguished sighs
of love and pain
and broken family ties
Their message meant nothing to me
I was just a child you see!

Today as I
hold photographs
in my hand
of children who
live in a distant land
I remember that message
now painfully clear
I am one with a woman
I never knew
I have paper children too!

Beatrice G. Davis

Nest

One day I saw
a cock-eyed robin, no Le Corbusier,
twig-weaving in the voluptuously drooping
wisteria vine right over the driveway.
Oh no, no place for a nest.
Why not the Indianapolis Speedway
or Broadway and 42nd Street?
Newsboys, mailmen, pollsters,
Bible sellers, curious dogs,
the huge brown truck from UPS.
Go away, not here, I said,
and even aimed the fine-spray hose
into the leafy filigree.
But the next day it was there,
solid, wedged and balanced,
a good job for a dumb robin.

One day
my daughter called from the hospital
to say, Fuck it, she was tired of it all
and wanted to die.

And then one day
there it was on the steaming blacktop,
the first unfledged to fall,
all feet and yellow beak and astonished eyes
in a limp, rotating head.
I had to drag the ladder from the shed
and lift the thing, gaping, screechless, terrified,
back up into its twiggery,
and sling a sheet between the vines
as safety net to catch
the next young brainless acrobat.

Joan Sevick

In the Grace

This time last year
pain drove the drugs down your throat
you in the way of a truck
you in the back seat with a car battery smashing
I numb but performing
spunk is all that's left us sometimes
"Kill for your mate
die for your children"
we would   we would
come up for a breath every three months or so
what was that?
I want a steelworker
working on my nerves and yours
connecting and encasing them in strong shine
but leaving the heart alone
that radiance only your eyes show

It's green on the land again
hope springs and I make my way
to the ocean we love
I didn't know that many tears
could run wave after wave
over and through this hunched shell
But it's okay . . . just okay
yet deep and good this feeling
like the peace at the bottom
where no fear is left
and I am held in a warm and watery place

Your smile is real most days now
clarity gains ground
your understanding, your courage
pour through the edges of a tight grip
on a life that's learning to sing again
to moan, to wail, to praise
to lock on as if you really knew
what happened and why
I like to stand in the grace of your smile.

Paddy Noble

Moving Day

Solomon chose an understanding heart.
God made him wise as well.
I fear I have too little wisdom,
too much understanding.

Your guidance counselor chided me for being too
understanding. That became a joke between us
when you'd get your way and when I did for you
what you should have done.

How hard to strike a balance. Letting go,
holding on, holding up, holding back.
I remember chaffing at my mother's fearful
cautions, tried not to pass them on to you.

When you were two I went with her to Israel.
At the Dead Sea the bus ran late, no time
for a bathing suit. I hiked my long skirt up my thighs —
started wading in —

"Patti, you'll get your skirt wet!" Mother shouted
from the bus. We laughed about that scene for years,
then I had a chance to play it back: Fifteen,
on your own in Jerusalem, you called from a bus station

when a girl invited you down to the seaside town of Eilat.
From the other side of the world I pushed away
the image of a bus strewn across the road
and said, "Go get your pants wet."

Moses and Jesus, standing on the shore
come to mind today. Turning to Moses,
Jesus asks how to do it, and Moses tells him,
"Walk on the rocks."

My rabbi taught me God's a metaphor
for God, said the Red Sea was a reed sea
and Moses knew the tides, making the passage
even more wonderful.

Find the solid places, slippery though they be —
life is washed with blood and tears.
Learn the tides.
Get your pants wet.

Patti Tana

Philosophy, Romance of the Aged

Philosophy, Romance of the Aged

before the angel of death
chooses me to say goodbye
to this body I use
this body that is beginning
to forsake me
this body that once belonged to another
is used
is old
this body of summers
on the beach
burned by sun
this body of winters
bruised by cold

before the angel of death
chooses me for that
final journey
I am getting fit
walking thirty minutes
a day
eating low-fat
low-tasting food
avoiding sun's
harmful rays
treading icy streets
cautiously
detaining death's angel
by a passion for life

Rita Katz

Ladybug

Ladybug, the autumnal, menopausal forest is aflame,
Burning with your yearning and desire: go home.
No season of mists or mellow fruitfulness for you, only
The hot flash of Eros dying, growing old.

Fall now, the deep loam envelops your breasts,
Dugs that hang low. The crimson leaves as
Veined as your hands, varices red and blue,
Glitter with last dew, the brilliance before death.

Can you, withered Phoenix, rise?
Female over fifty, do you have your music too?

Larissa Shmailo

My Song

It has been many years
since the maestro resplendent
in velvet opera cape
said the words to two small girls
in white pinafores,
"Your mother has the voice of an angel."

This evening I stand in the choir loft
my cape draping a chair
my voice floating
through Schubert's score in the hushed
reverence of the church
like the sound of angels rising

Lorraine Mund

Photo of the Artist

The strong face of Georgia O'Keefe
peers from under black felt
cowboy hat perched above her brow.

Eyes moist with moonlight and
ideas, she gathers bones
that will grow flesh.

Skull born on white canvas
ghost of a long-ago barren time
lonely hours stretching to the desert.

Tinted photo from the past
trapped in paint, pinned to a board,
a white rose grows inside her petals.

Fran Redbell Bolinder

The Painters

The painters come
with their cans and brushes and rollers
to cover the lost colors
years have resolved to a wistful shadow
of what might have been.

I selected whites this time,
shades of purity,
searching for my truth
in the tenuousness
of untrammeled snow
in its moment in
the melting sun.

The painters come
and my artifacts huddle together
beneath splattered drop cloths
and I wonder who
did a room in midnight blue
and who in sharp citrus yellow
and who in peachy pink.
I wonder at the hope behind
the rainbow colors.

I huddle with the artifact
in a dark void of silence,
lacking the passion of midnight blue,
citrus yellow, peachy pink.

They tell me, these painters,
it will be bold
when it is done.
I know
it is only
the blank page
to be won.

Barbara Novack

What Is Sufficient

One room: a window facing east,
sunlight on the table where I sit thinking
how time moves so slowly as I age,
as I read, slowly, entering the text,
sunlight on my neck
penetrates the network of small bone.

I would like to see you, speak with you,
before I'm finished reading,
before the sunlight fades
to vacant shadow and I fall asleep,
someone else inhabiting the room, reading,
words on the page arranged into a story,

your story, my story, your room, my room,
the first and last the only
true commitment.

Pat Falk

Last Call

The last time we spoke
you heard a knock at your door
and said, "Gotta go —
I'll call you back," but didn't,
and I thought you were brushing me off.

Years later I left you a message
that our friend had been killed
suddenly in a car crash
without a moment's grace to say
farewell to his wife and daughter

and your sister called me back
to say you'd been dead for years,
hadn't even seen the Towers fall,
and isn't it strange
how so much could happen
without your knowing.

From time to time
I think about our last call
and what I might have said
if I had known death
was knocking at your door.

Patti Tana

The Dance I Did Not Know

Now I understand the dance between reality and illusion.
It's quite simple. Reality never gives up. It can't be
willed away with whines and whispers, swept away with
slurs or shouts. Side steps and pratfalls make no dent
at all since it's unrelenting in its measure of time.

On the other hand, my illusions are conjured at will.
I put down anger on a park bench and walk away.
I collect the world in small handfuls and release them
to the wind. I close my eyes and still feel the ocean's
pulse breathe in and out the tide. Even my loved ones
who've danced death's final waltz are whole again
despite reality's need to lay their graves at my feet.

Sasha Ettinger

Confession

We have become invisible
Years ago walking
Past men in trucks
Men working high on girders
Whistles followed us

We miss the whistles
That gave voice
To our ease of stride
The flash of unhooded eyes

We have become invisible
Adornments lost to wrinkles
And sensible shoes

In the winter of our lives
We are at home within ourselves
We look beyond the mirror

At night when the fire is banked
We let down our hair
Dreams steam from our heart

Beverly Pion

Two Moons

My left breast looks like a moon
in partial eclipse.

Looking at the glass
half full
I see it is a lifesaver,
the part that's missing
making room for me to hold on
to the part that lives.

When I was a child
I would rest my head
on my mother's ample pillows.

Now my head sinks
into my comfortable bed,
and my body
whole
turns to the side

the right full moon and the left
rising and falling with breath

Patti Tana

Anatomy

sometimes my heart is a stone
my eyes are coals
my mouth is a trap
my legs leaden sacks

in my brain there's a storm
the pressure of a halo
a burning current
but my hands lift

flowers into vases
draw curtains, erase
grease spots, wash
windows, design

delicate concoctions
to feed the beast, the bully
the body, the burden
the chassis, the frame.

Claire Nicolas White

Cole Bay at Twilight

needles of rain prick evening winds
toss crushed soda bottles, decomposed paper boxes
into patterns suffocating the beach
bellies of gray clouds gather
over dimming mountains sheltering Cole Bay
threaten to burst their bladders over moored sailboats
looking frail and thin, sails furling the mast
black streaks pierce the sky momentarily
paralyzing Ruth on her daily walk across twilight
she kicks coffee-stained cups scattered on sand
abused by storms, neglected by man
then she runs into the water for a final swim
before losing another day
before the inevitable dark

Joan Magiet

Misplaced Memories

I did not throw them out
They are not gone.
They are only hiding in some secret place
Like mischievous children
Lingering in their hiding places
Long after the game ends,
"Come out, come out, wherever you are!"

It isn't like the loss of solid things
The kinds of things you put away and find
Or throw out in the trash when they are worn
Beyond their use and can no longer serve.

Those things can be managed and set right,
Replaced, perhaps, if they cannot be found.
But memories that vanish out of sight
Have no replacement in the tattered mind.

Yet I seek them as if they were of wood
Or steel or like some other solid thing.
Their lack of form and order make me cry
But tears do not summon them back to life.
Though I know I did not throw them out
The weary brain cannot escape its maze
Nor make them likely to be found.

So slowly, I must set these thoughts aside,
For children will grow tired of their game
And come back out when evening starts to fall.
Things misplaced will suddenly appear.
Perhaps at first they'll come out one by one
And fill the empty spaces once again.
The sun that rises will again bring dawn,
For I did not throw them out —
They are not gone.

Margaret Dinzlet Shaw

The Plot

Book discussions are the rage
But if you don't read every page
Or if a passage you forget
Then you may certainly regret
You ever joined this group.
You feel like such a nincompoop
As all too glibly they refer
To when and where, or him and her,
Plot twists you just can't recall
And you didn't like the book at all!
So how to turn the next one down?
Whatever the date, be out of town!

Muriel Lilker

Aging Remedy

I've decided
to stop counting birthdays;
next year I'll turn 52
again.

54 will be 51.
At 55 I'll celebrate my 50th
with my kid sister,
secretly take myself
out on the town.

65 will be 40,
75, 30.

At 85, 20...
I'll buy a tie-dye dress
braid my hair
blast Jethro Tull
paint a peace sign on my forehead
put flowers in my hair,
dance barefoot around the backyard
in a mid-April's spring rain.

At 95
green plaid uniform
ice skating
Beatles.
Collect a sticker for each library book read.

If I make it to 100,
old reruns of the Little Rascals,
Bowery Boys, Charlie Chan,
watch Abbott and Costello
meet Frankenstein
on a black and white TV.
I'll find a small tree
to climb

children to play with.

Kathleen Donnelly

Dialogue

"I didn't expect to die so young," she said
"What does she mean? She's seventy-five if she's a day
That's no spring chicken I would say"

"Who do you see, young man in your white coat
Stethoscope dangling from your tan unwattled neck,
Some battered, life-tossed human wreck?

"Look past the wrinkled skin, you'll find
A girl in saddle shoes, boyfriend in hand
Still jitterbugging to Glen Miller's band

"These narrow, dry and withered lips you wet
Retain the thrilling pressure yet of love's first kiss
The brush of babies' silken skin, all this

"Is fresh within this husk containing me
A wild, impassioned, ardent youth
An eager seeker after truth"

The young man's stethoscope, a dowser's wand,
Glides back and forth across the concave chest
Searches, listens, comes to rest

Marilyn Goldsmith

"A Life Unlived Is Not Worth Examining"*

Dog food,
weeds in the dahlia bed,
Jeopardy at seven, *News* at eleven,
skimming *Scientific American* for something
I can understand,
participating in the cosmic idea
only so far as the earth turns,
the universe expands, and I'm
a fellow traveler.

There is a man working on his third memoir.
Maybe he forgot something,
one of his wives,
or realized he misunderstood his mother.
But he is a celebrity
and every event is a commodity.
You will remember him.
I could ghostwrite my own life and lie.
Perhaps I will die in some dramatic and significant way.
But then, death is not an event in one's life.
There is only the aromatic slime of kibble and liver chunks,
the primal appeal of wet peat between fingers,
and the lilac look of a spring morning
while I'm still here.

Joan Sevick

*Robert Hughs reviewing a boring memoir

The Garden

The Garden

The iron gate leading in from the street
is locked.
The woman looks through it
into a landscape:
Fountain, pool, irises,
and at the far end
where light thickens like water
a girl sitting under a tree,
hair rippled by the shadows of leaves.

The woman shouts to her:
Don't marry him —
There's another life
waiting for us.

The column of water
shatters into splinters of light.

The iris opens too wide.
Spill of saffron petals
on black water.

The girl looks up and sees
through the bars of the gate
the face of her unborn child

Barbara Lucas

Kitchen Privileges

My pocket holds the seeds I plant
I tear their envelopes neatly
remembering another tearing and the birth of our son
you planted so well, my darling
placed your ear to the soft ground of my belly
to hear your children grow

I drop the seeds two by two
so if one is not ripe the other will be
have more than one child, mother said
these pale shells will crack open
shoot little green hands above a lip of soil
and pray for rain
I can cope with the garden
it's people I can't weed out of my life

Down season the vines will bear fruit
they'll spread a canopy of leaves
under which will live a universe
mulching and munching the dead
I'll watch for the aphid, the beetle, the cutworm
destroy my work if I let them, destroy my children
I'll pinch out their life between my fingers
and, like a murderer, wear gloves

I lay down straw between the rows
put my garden to bed
till the melons and squash and the cucumber
all have heads big enough for the table
and the table is still big enough for the children
that I have fed and laughed and cried over
coming home now when they want to, because it's there
and the kitchen's a warm place to remember in

I'll soak in a tub and return to my growing tomorrow
or maybe tonight in the moonlight
when I can whisper alone to the garden
that what I'd really like
is to lie down in the fall with the pumpkins
and get planted again in the spring.

Paddy Noble

Omens of Passing

It isn't just because they're gone I weep,
The old tree loses leaves each fall yet lives.
The new spring brings new buds of blossoms sweet
That in the summertime will be complete.

Then fruits will come from summer's warm caress,
The tree rejoicing in the birth it gives.
What vast creative powers it does possess
With autumn leaves of splendor to impress.

But I have seen the old trees bend and die
A slow death when the roots are choked of breath
And bark splits open wide as if to sigh
And slender branch no longer seeks the sky.

It isn't just because they're gone I bleed.
If roots are torn asunder, too soon death
Will steal sway the cradle of the seed
And swallow up tomorrow in its greed.

Margaret Dinzler Shaw

Woman with Scissors, Deadheading Poppies

Villanelle

Each faded blossom bending, row on row,
Receives a cut that forces further red.
Though they're beheaded, magic makes them grow.

. . .

She plants black seeds each spring, and some self-sow
To die by heavy hand that halts their spread,
No errant plant extending past its row.

Unfurled in June, her crimson poppies blow.
She lops off wilted flowers, feels no dread
In calling them "deadheaded": Still they grow.

Bright sun on soil plus moisture seal the slow
Regeneration sinking through the bed
Of blood-red hopefuls mending, row on row.

. . .

A second blooming comes; prophets say so.
Late flowers offer proof — at least a shred:
On our deathbeds, a Master makes his show.

Can autumn gardens help us suffer woe?
Do headless horsemen lead us by a thread?
Are souls ascending, row by rigid row?
Though we're death-headed, grace make us regrow.

Barbara Horn

On My Eightieth Birthday

I want a flowery dress of slinky silk
bursting with tropical blossoms,
purple and fuchsia hibiscus cascading
over breasts in such abundance everyone will say,
"Ahhh, the Hanging Gardens of Babylon!"

I want young vines to entwine my waist
slide over my hips in green ecstasy
ribbon out with each hip's sway
shimmy with each thigh's thrust.

I want to strut past the Senior Center
where the guys will throw down their canes
and walkers and bump into each other
as they rush to inhale my flowers.

I want tiger lilies, oleander, bougainvillea,
orchids growing along the hem
blooming in a collision of chaotic colors
with each step I take.

And my feet will dance in that garden
to the song I'm singing
and the ruffles on my skirt will bounce and flirt
as I swing my hips to a jazzy beat
and sing and sing and sing!

Muriel Harris Weinstein

Bringing in Tomatoes

The tomatoes, they are late this year,
As I was late in planting.
The seasons seem to fly so fast,
I just cannot keep up to last.

The tomatoes on my plate this year
Are just a little wanting.
Their flavor weaker than I'd wish.
They're not the main course on my dish.

My children did not care or see
For they were gone last season.
Their empty chair, the empty plate,
Give me no need to cultivate.

So this year I planted only three
For change dictates the reason.
They take their time. They seem to know
I do not want to watch them grow.

Bringing in tomatoes then
Was summer's sweet tradition.
Now that it's postponed to fall
It might not mean much after all.

But if I miss the bringing when
It's always been my mission,
It might make sense next year to sow
A better crop and watch them grow.

Margaret Dinzler Shaw

Post Humus

Scatter my ashes in my garden
so I can be near my loves.
Say a few honest words,
sing a gentle song,
join hands in a circle of flesh.
Please tell some stories
about me making you laugh.
I love to make you laugh.

When I've had time to settle
and green gathers into buds,
remember I love blossoms
bursting in spring.
As the season ripens
remember my persistent passion.

And if you come in my garden
on an August afternoon,
pluck a bright red globe,
let juice run down your chin
and the seeds stick to your cheek.

When I'm dead I want folks to smile
and say, "That Patti, she sure is
some tomato!"

Patti Tana

Crow Garden

Do I remember
what it was like
before I agreed to be human?

Before the angels
came to me
offering me another chance
to dwell in flesh,
to experience desire.

Sitting in my garden
the rusty wrought iron table
reminds me how perishable
things are on this earth.

The center hole
that should hold the umbrella
casting shade so I wouldn't have to squint
heaves up and separates from the table.
The yellow umbrella we forgot
to store inside for the winter
discarded, gone to mold and mildew.

I watch my hands,
my nails uncharacteristically polished pink.
An insistent crow my company,
his voice loud,
his body hidden within trees.

The cosmos taller
than I could have imagined,
rugged but beautiful
in their own shades of pink,
lead me quietly back
to those angels and their promises:

    this time I would do it right,
    this time the flesh would be a pleasure
    not a burden,
    that I would choose wisely
    and negotiate fate.

My small angels just inside
home from camp today
each for their own reason
implicated in these memories:

    Mia tells stories
    of her time before time;
    David meets angels
    in his dreams.

Is it true that I created their flesh?
Was it sin or blessing
to invite their souls
to join me in this garden
of rusting iron, gargantuan cosmos,
crow sounds.

Laurel Brett

Coda: Seasoned

Seasoned

This poem is too young to get past the bouncer at the door.
This poem is just a child,
hasn't lived for much more than a page.
This poem is seasoned with the words of mocking children.
This poem has met with angry fists of the prejudice
of high school halls.

This poem has lived on city streets, slept on someone's sofa,
delivered newspapers, and collected cans.
This poem is written with a tempered hand, a tattered heart.
This poem is written with the scars of more
than just an average life.
This poem is seasoned with a mother's terminal cancer,
a father's broken heart, taped and mended
with a porcine skin, but far from repair.

This poem has seen through eyes once sharp as eagle's,
vision now blurred with task and time.
This poem knows the pain of a wounded womb
and battered bones.
This poem has known the pleasure of a gentle man.

This poem is not eligible for Medicare.
This poem struggles to swim in big fish waters
floating to the surface.
This poem is not a poem at all.

Yolanda Coulaz

About the Poets & Acknowledgments

SUSAN ASTOR has taught poetry in public schools and libraries for over twenty-five years. Her poems appear in *The Paris Review, The Partisan Review, Poet Lore,* and elsewhere. Susan is the author of *Dame* (University of Georgia Press, 1980) and *Spider Lies* (Trumble Press, 2003), which includes the four poems in this anthology.

BARBARA BARNARD is Coordinator of the Creative Writing Project and advisor of the student literary magazine *Luna* at Nassau Community College. Winner of the *Nassau Review* Poetry Award (2002), she also writes book reviews, edited the textbook *Access Literature* (2006), and has just completed a novel. "Wolf Season" was published in *Eclipse.*

FRAN RADBELL BOLINDER co-authored *Lightcatchers* and edited the "Stone Hinge" column for The Nassau Mineral Club. Her poems have won awards from The Shelley Society of New York and the New York Poetry Forum.

MALLIE E. BOMAN, playwright, filmmaker, and performing artist, is featured in her award-winning play *Mona Lisa, Budda & Me* and on the CD *Kokoro Kara.* She has been artist-in-residence at Taliesin East and is currently directing and producing a documentary film *The Thing Itself* on visionary poet George Bruce.

SHARON BOURKE has poems in *Understanding the New Black Poetry, Celebrations, Children of Promise,* and *Poetry Magazine.* See her art at sharonbourke. womanmade.net. and read more poems at sharonbourkewritings.net. "How Many Wars" appeared on-line at Poets Against the War.org.

LAUREL BRETT teaches Mythology at Suffolk Community College, English and Women's Studies at Nassau Community College, and Asian Studies at Stony Brook. She has published poems and essays in various venues and is currently completing her first novel.

BERNADINE BROWN has taught in the English Department at Nassau Community College since 1969.

PAULA CAMACHO, author of *Hidden Between Branches, November's Diary,* and *The Short Lives of Giants,* moderates the Farmingdale Poetry Group. Paula is Chair of the Nassau County Poet Laureate Panel. "Sister Shaman" was published in *Lucidity.*

GAIL CHAPMAN enjoys teaching English at Nassau Community College, especially Shakespeare's comedies and histories. "Astronomy Lesson" and "Those Saturday Nights" were published in the *Nassau Review.* "Those Saturday Nights" also appeared in the first issue of *Long Island Quarterly* in 1990.

YOLANDA COULAZ is founder of the Purple Sage Press, editor of *For Loving Precious Beast* (2006), and author of *Spirits and Oxygen* (2003). "Seasoned" won second in the 2007 Farmingdale Poetry Group Contest, and her signature poem "Cool, Cotton Comfort" won the Mattia Family 8th International Poetry Competition.

BEATRICE G. DAVIS, author of *Looking Out With an Inner Eye*, is a retired language arts teacher who writes poems and educational materials. "Paper Children" appeared in *North Shore Woman's Newspaper, Lucidity,* and *Crystal Rainbow.*

KATHALEEN DONNELLY, a Nurse Practitioner in Cardiology at Stony Brook University Hospital, has had poems published in the *Literary Review* and *Long Island Quarterly.*

SALLY ANN DRUCKER teaches English at Nassau Community College and her poems have been widely published. "Washday" rode the buses of Buffalo as a "Poetry on the Buses" contest winner. "Eve's Song" was published in her *Walking the Desert Lion* (Ena Press, 1984).

SASHA ETTINGER, mother of four, grandmother of eight, is a former diagnostician and special education teacher. She is an active participant in Max Wheat's Tap Roots workshop, George Wallace's Hutton House workshop, and Gladys Henderson's Port Washington workshop.

NATASHA MARIA EWART loves animals and is studying Animal Science at Pennsylvania State University. Her parents are from Kingston, Jamaica, and her father has been her inspiration. "Black Beauty" is part of the collaborative performance *Diary of a Mad Black Feminist.*

PAT FALK, author of the poetry collections *In the Shape of a Woman* and *Crazy Jane,* editor of *Sighting: Poems on Discovery,* teaches writing, literature, and Women's Studies at Nassau Community College. Her poems have received awards from The National League of American Pen Women, *Black Bear Review, Many Mountains Moving,* and the *Pushcart Press.*

DIANA FESTA, author of *Arches to the West, Ice Sparrow, Thresholds,* and *Bedrock,* also writes literary criticism and is the recipient of a Guggenheim Fellowship and the Guizot Award from the French Academy.

MARILYN GOLDSMITH is a former English teacher. Encouraged by attendance at Taproot Writer's Workshops, she has recently returned to writing. Marilyn has two grown children and a husband who form a loud, noisy cheering squad.

LYNN GREEN is a journalist, business writer, and screenplay writer/producer. Her poems were featured in the Asbury Short Film Show; her poetry book *Whispers in the Sand* is forthcoming. "Double Nickels I" and "Double Nickels II" appeared in *River Voices.*

MARY GUND is an artist who has worked in the Metropolitan Museum of Art framing department. The greatest joy of her life is becoming a mother.

Gladys Henderson, artist, poet, teacher, and retired retail executive, leads poetry workshops at the Graphic Eye Gallery in Port Washington and for Live Poets in Islip, and she co-hosts poetry readings at Cool Beanz. "Pieta" appeared in *Kaleidoscope* and "Wading the Tidal Pools" in *PPA Literary Review* (2005).

Mary Himmelweit, who speaks four languages and can communicate in four more, finds writing poetry the perfect medium to make a long story short. She has studied economics and behavioral psychology, is a mother of two, teaches ESL, and welds steel sculptures.

Katherine A. Hogan is a professor in the LIU-Brooklyn Higher Education Opportunity Program. Her poems, short stories, and plays have won prizes and have been performed.

Barbara Horn is a personal essayist, member of Women Writing Women's Lives, and Coordinator of Women's Studies at Nassau Community College. Born in rural Missouri, she writes about pioneer and working-class women. Many of her essays, reviews of women writers, and afterwards for Dorothy Bryant novels have been published.

Kathrine Jason edited and translated *Name and Tears: Forty Years of Italian Fiction* and the stories of Tommaso Landolfi. She is a professor of English at Nassau Community College. Her poems have been published in *The New Yorker* and elsewhere. "Return of My Father" was published in *Poetry Magazine*.

Evelyn Kandel is a visual artist who began including poems in her artwork and the poetry became more important than the art. She hosts Performance Poets Association readings, and has had poems published in the *Long Island Quarterly*, *PPA Literary Journal*, and *Taproot Journal*.

Rita Katz is an artist whose work is in the permanent collection at Nassau Community College and is the author of five books. Her poetry has won awards and has appeared in the *Long Island Quarterly* and the *Long Island Review*.

Andrea Kaufman grew up on Minneapolis where she became a member of The Nancy Hauser Modern Dance Company. After raising four children, she went to college and is now a high school English teacher. Currently Andrea is writing a biography of Nancy Hauser.

Beverly E. Kotch went to college at fifty after her children were grown and is now Director of Program Development for the Long Island Writer's Guild. Her poems have received awards and she holds a scholarship key in history from Phi Alpha Theta.

Mindy Kronenberg is Director of Academic Support Service at SUNY Empire State College and editor of *Book/Mark Quarterly Review*. "My Mother's Fruitbowl" and "Circular Motion" are in her *Dismantling the Playground* (Birnham Wood Graphics, 1991). Mindy's *Gravity of Desire* is forthcoming.

MURIEL LILKER wrote the "Who Says Life Is Easy" column in the *Times Ledger* and has had poems in *Good Housekeeping, Reader's Digest,* and *The World Street Journal.* "The Plot" appeared in the "Metropolitan Diary" of *The New York Times.*

BARBARA LUCAS is a professor of English at Nassau Community College and former editor of *Xanadu* and Director of the Poetry Society of America on Long Island. Her poems have appeared in numerous journals, including the *Beloit Poetry Journal, Kansas Quarterly,* and *Windlass Orchard.*

BEDA LYON, a mother of two and grandmother of four, taught English and had ten years of joy teaching preschool children.

JOAN MAGIET is a college English teacher and award-winning journalist who hosts poetry readings at B&N in Manhasset. She is a Reiki Master who practices Reiki in her daily life. Joan's travels inspire her to write.

MARIA MANOBIANCO is an artist and the author of *Between Ashes and Flame* (2005). She was awarded Outstanding Adult Student of Poetry (2004) by the Farmingdale School District and other awards.

JOHANNA MASTROTOTARO developed creative writing courses for Lifelong Learning at Nassau Community College where she teaches Women's Studies. Johanna is a member of the Long Island Writing Project, and she is completing her poetry book *Mourning Song* and a creative writing workbook.

MARCIA MCNAIR, former assistant editor at *Essence Magazine,* teaches African American Literature at Molloy College and Journalism at Nassau Community College. She is author of the nonfiction story *Before We Were Gangstas* and the collaborative performance *Diary of a Mad Black Feminist,* which includes "Long Island Just Isn't Long Enough."

SUSAN MELCHIOR, author of *Your Home and Mine* (1987) and *Soup of Our Dreams* (1993), taught writing and theater in Pt. Washington for years, then combined these passions into the Long Island Poetry Theater. Susan continues her poetry theater in Cooperstown, New York, and Apollo Beach, Florida.

LORRAINE MUND decided three years ago to return to one of her passions, singing, and has been singing operatic arias and classical songs in local venues. Since 1974 she has taught English in Long Island colleges and currently teaches at Nassau Community College. You can hear Lorraine sing on her CD *Avid Diva.*

GLORIA G. MURRAY'S poems have appeared in Ted Kooser's online column *American Life in Poetry, Poet Lore, The Paterson Review, Jewish Women's Literary Annual 2003, Bitterroot, Long Island Quarterly,* and other journals.

PADDY NOBLE has won poetry awards and her poems are widely published, including in *The Light of City and Sea* and *Long Island Sound Anthology.* "Kitchen Privileges" was published in her *Kitchen Privileges* and "In The Grace" in her *From the Outside In.*

BARBARA NOVACK is Writer-in-Residence at Molloy College where she teaches English. In addition to writing three collections of poetry and conducting writers' workshops, she has written novels and a book of historical biographies. "Thaw" appeared in *Nassau Review* and "The Painters" in *The Cape Rock*.

LINDA OPYR has been published in *The Hudson Review, The Atlanta Review,* and *The New York Times.* Her work was honored by a Suffolk County Legislature Proclamation in 2001. Linda is the author of six collections of poetry, most recently *If We Are What We Remember* (Whittier Publications, Inc., 2005), which includes "I See Your Face," "No Moon," and "Blood Sisters."

BEVERLY PION is a retired teacher, mother of two, grandmother of five, who loves to garden, read, and write.

MARCIA SILVERBERG PULEWITZ grew up in the Bronx where she cooked with her mother Rose and Grandma Becky. "Talim for My Brother" won first prize in the C. W. Post Poetry Contest. She is the Family Liaison/Membership Administrator at AHRC Nassau. Marcia graduated from Hofstra at fifty-nine.

BARBARA REIHER-MEYERS, author of *Sounds Familiar* (2005) and editor of several volumes of poetry, is a board member of the Long Island Poetry Collective. She has coordinated events for the Northport Arts Coalition and Smithtown Township Arts Council, and she also curates the poetry calendar www.poetz.com/longisland.

ELLEN POBER RITTBERG, mother of three, loves nature, art, theater, and good cinema. Her poems have appeared in the *Kansas Quarterly, Long Island Quarterly,* and have won the Borders Bookstore poetry contest. "Consider the Constellations" appeared in *Flutter.*

RUTH SABATH ROSENTHAL has poems in *Voices Israel* anthology and literary magazines, including *Connecticut Review, Mobius–The Poetry Magazine. Ibbetson Street,* which nominated "on yet another birthday" for a Pushcart Prize, published "For Want of Red," "I Ate My Mother's Hair," and "Riding Past the Museum." Hear Ruth's poems at her website ruthsabathrosenthal.moonfruit.com.

JENNIFER ROSOFF is a painter, poet, chiropractor, and acupuncturist who lives in Brookhaven with her cat and two dogs. Her poem "The Pack" is included in *For Loving Precious Beast* (Purple Sage Press, 2006), ed. Yolanda Coulaz.

NARGES ROTHERMEL, whose parents are Russian and Turkish, was born in Persia where she established and directed a school for LPNs. Since 1969 she has practiced nursing in the U. S. As a child she started writing poetry in Farsi, but when she was diagnosed with breast cancer in 1978 she decided to write in English "so my children could read and know me if I didn't survive." Narges is a poet and a survivor.

JOAN SEVICK, Professor of English at Nassau Community College, has been published in *The Mississippi Review, Crosscurrents, Confrontation,* and the *Anthology of Chester H. Jones Poetry Competition Winners. Nassau Review* published "A Life Unlived Is Not Worth Examining" and "Nest." "Nest" also appeared in *Poets On: Ripening.*

ROCHELLE JEWEL SHAPIRO teaches "Writing the Personal Essay" at UCLA online, and she reviews fiction, nonfiction, and poetry. Her essays, short stories, and poems have appeared in *Newsweek, The Iowa Review,* and *Negative Capability,* and her novel *Miriam the Medium* (2004) was nominated for the Harold U. Ribelow Award.

INES SENNA SHAW lives in Long Beach, NY. She first wrote poems in English at age twelve in Rio de Janeiro, Brazil, where she lived until twenty-one. She has kept her poetry private throughout the years, but at this stage of her life she feels comfortable sharing it.

MARGARET DINZLER SHAW is founder of the Lamberson Corona Press, former columnist for *Reading Today,* photographer, painter, and professor in the Department of Reading and Basic Education at Nassau Community College. She published a novel and, in collaboration with her late mother, a book of poems. The poems in this anthology will be in her book *Ordinary Days.*

LARISSA SHMAILO translated the Russian Futurist opera *Victory over the Sun* by A. Kruchenych, and founded the reading series *Sliding Scale Poetry* and the poetry association *The Feminist Poets in Low-Cut Blouses.* "Williamsburg Poem" appeared in *Rattapallax.* You can hear Larissa read her poems on her *The No-Net World* CD (2006) at http://cdbaby.com/cd/shmailo.

SISTA GIRL (REV. GAIL HALIBURTON) is an African-American griot (GREE-oh), a storyteller-keeper of oral history, personification of all the griot spirits who came before her. She is Assistant Pastor at Trinity Temple Church in Brooklyn, a member of the *I Am Poetry Ensemble,* and was awarded a Long Island Council of the Arts grant in 2006 for her one-woman show "A History of Us." Sista Girl collaborated on *Diary of a Mad Black Feminist* and she performs her poem "Yesterday" in the play.

GAIL TELLER teaches English at Hofstra University and is the Director of the Plainview Mid-Island Y Poetry Series. Author of *One Small Kindness, Moving Day, Shorehaven,* and *At the Intersecton of Everything You Have Ever Loved,* she conducts many workshops, and her poems have been published widely and won numerous awards.

PRAMILA VENKATESWARAN, author of *Thirtha* (Yuganta Press, 2002) and essays in *The Women's Studies Quarterly* and *Language Crossings,* was a finalist for the Allen Ginsberg Poetry Award and performed her poems most recently in the Geraldine R. Dodge Festival. Pramila teaches English and Women's Studies at Nassau Community College.

MURIEL HARRIS WEINSTEIN received the 1990 *Nassau Review* poetry award. *When Louis Armstrong Taught Me Scat,* her children's picture book, is forthcoming from Chronicle Publishers.

BEVERLY WEISMAN is an attorney who teaches in the Writing Center at Nassau Community College. Though this is her first poetry publication in English, she has won prizes for the poems she has written in French.

CLAIRE NICOLAS WHITE, author of *Riding at Anchor, Biography and Other Poems,* the novel *The Death of the Orange Trees,* a memoir *Fragments of Stained Glass,* and a family history *The Elephant and the Rose.* She has also translated three novels from the Dutch and poetry from French and Dutch.

PATTI TANA is Professor of English at Nassau Community College and Associate Editor of the *Long Island Quarterly.* She is the author of seven books of poetry, most recently *Make Your Way Across This Bridge: New & Selected Writings* (Whittier Publications, Inc., 2003) and *This Is Why You Flew Ten Thousand Miles* (Whittier Publications, Inc., 2006). Her poems in this anthology are from these two books, and they were first published in the *Nassau Review,* edited by Paul Doyle.

Patti's poem "Post Humus" has been read at celebrations of life since it appeared in *When I Am an Old Woman I Shall Wear Purple* (1987), edited by Sandra Martz. Listen to Patti read "Post Humus," "Because," "Skin Knows Skin" and other poems at www.pattitana.com.

E. WILLA HAAS is a psychotherapist and family therapist in Sea Cliff, New York. She is the author of *Divorce Ghosts: Connected Short Stories & Novella* (2006), and the forthcoming *Maury Mandlebaum's Cookbook for Single Men*, a humorous photo-illustrated cookbook, and *Sunday is Daddy's Day,* a children's book dedicated to helping divorced parents speak with young children. Her screenplay *Burt's Boy* is in pre-production. View a list of her other projects at www.quadrasoul.com.

E. Willa is president of Quadrasoul Publishing & Production Company. *Songs of Seasoned Women* is the child of her imagination.